People of the Past

Contents

Features

What do we mean when we refer to "prehistory"? Find out on page 5.

Wonderful ancient paintings have been found on the walls of some caves. Learn more about them on page 7.

In a Stone Age village, sometimes even the furniture was made from stone! Read about Skara Brae in **Stone Age Lifestyle** on page 16.

How do scientists discover the age of an ancient artifact? Check your idea on page 23.

Who were the first people in North America?
Visit www.rigbyinfoquest.com
for more about **PREHISTORIC PEOPLE.**

Life Before History

Today, many people take food and comfortable housing for granted, but life has not always been this easy. Long ago, people spent all their time simply staying alive!

Most scientists believe that early people lived more than two million years ago. However, the first human beings that looked like we do lived only about 160,000 years ago. From that time until about 10000 B.C., their way of life seems to have changed very little. Whatever these early people needed, they had to find a way of providing for themselves. People discovered that they needed to work together to survive. Banding together for protection was the first sign of the beginning of life as we know it.

WORD BUILDER

The word *prehistory* means "before history." We use this word to refer to the time before writing was invented about 5,000 years ago. Once writing was invented, human history could be recorded. Fossils provide much of what we know about prehistory.

Cave Life

Prehistoric people lived in a variety of places. Some lived under overhanging rocks, while others built huts of animal skins. Some people were lucky enough to find shelter in empty caves. Caves were valued because they provided some protection from dangerous animals.

Cave dwellers only left their caves to hunt and gather food. They ate meat and fish year-round, but the rest of their diet was linked to the seasons. There were berries and other fruits in summer, but food was not easy to find in winter. During this season, cave dwellers had to dig roots and often settle for dried meat, dried fruit, and nuts.

Prehistoric people made shelters with what they could find. This hut is made of animal bones and hides.

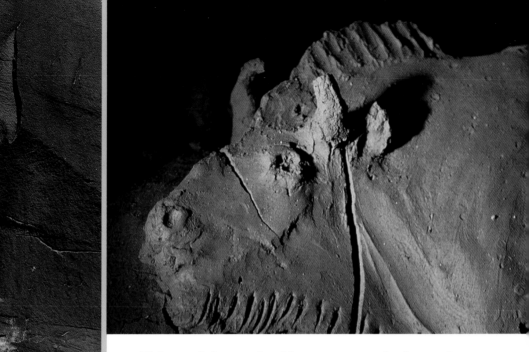

This sculpture of a bison was made from clay about 14,000 years ago in what is now France.

The oldest cave paintings yet discovered are 65,000 years old! Prehistoric people mainly used the colors black, red, and yellow, which they got from substances such as charcoal and clay. The deer, horses, and lions painted by prehistoric people are still familiar to us today, but aurochs, a kind of ox, and some other animals have become extinct.

The Power of Fire

Fire, and how to control it, was the most important discovery of prehistoric times. People had long known about fires that occurred naturally, usually through lightning strikes, but they had lived for generations without knowing how to start or control fire.

About 500,000 years ago, very early humans discovered that a spark from a stone called flint could start a fire in dry leaves. From that time on, people had the ability to cook their food, provide light for their caves, and warm cold nights. Fire was also a good method of keeping dangerous animals away.

Flint, a hard rock, was important to prehistoric people. It was not only used to start fires. Prehistoric people also used flint to make sharp tools and weapons.

Early Tools

Prehistoric people invented simple tools that were keys to their survival. They made cutting and drilling tools from stone and animal bones. They crafted spearheads and knives made of flint. Archaeologists have also found harpoons and fish spears at prehistoric sites. Along with these tools, large numbers of animal bones have been found, showing that prehistoric people were skilled in using the tools to hunt and fish.

One of the most important inventions from about 20,000 years ago was the needle! People were then able to sew animal skins together to make well-fitting clothing. This was vital to surviving freezing **ice age** winters.

TIME LINK

The Old Stone Age (also called the Paleolithic period) lasted from when people first used stones as rough tools, about two million years ago, to about 12,000 years ago. The Middle Stone Age, or Mesolithic period, then lasted until about 10,000 years ago. The New Stone Age, or Neolithic period, started when people began to farm and ended when people learned how to make tools from metal, about 6,000 years ago.

Spear made of deer bone with flint set in carved grooves

Dagger with point made of deer antler

Harpoon made of wood

The carving on the left is of a mammoth and made from a mammoth tusk. Mammoths had enormous tusks and were covered in shaggy hair. They became extinct about 11,000 years ago.

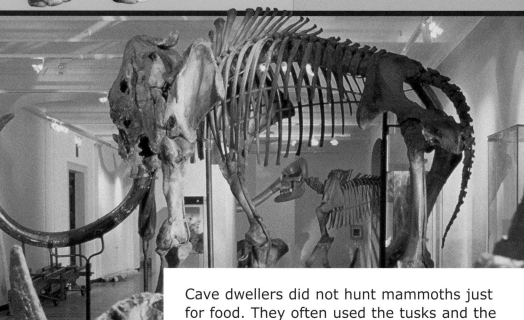

Cave dwellers did not hunt mammoths just for food. They often used the tusks and the bones to make tools and weapons.

On the Move

There are different opinions about the movement of prehistoric people. Many researchers believe that the earliest people lived in East Africa because that is where the earliest fossils have been found. It is thought people began to migrate from there to Asia and then Europe. People migrated for different reasons. Some were searching for a better food source and others were looking for a better environment. Some were forced to move by rival tribes.

As early as 65,000 years ago, people used boats to reach Australia. People began to colonize the Pacific Islands about 20,000 years ago. Most scientists believe people were living in North America by 15–20,000 years ago, having traveled on foot from Siberia into Alaska. Gradually, people populated South America as well.

This trail of fossilized footprints found in Tanzania is 3.6 million years old!

Early people reached North America at a time when ocean water levels were much lower than today because much of the water was frozen glacial ice. At that time, the Bering Strait was dry and formed a land bridge between Siberia and Alaska.

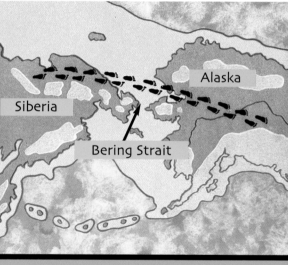

Siberia

Alaska

Bering Strait

Early people probably traveled from island to island in dugout canoes. A dugout canoe is made by scooping out the inside of a whole tree trunk. Some cultures still make dugout canoes today as shown at left.

From Hunting to Farming

Hunters and Gatherers

For thousands of years, prehistoric people relied totally on hunting animals and gathering wild fruit and vegetables. Usually, men were the hunters and women were the gatherers. Their lives were difficult. Hunters often had to travel long distances to find food. When food was scarce, whole families had to move to a new location.

Families were small, and everyone needed to be able to walk long distances. This was difficult for very young children and the elderly, and they often died on journeys. For many centuries, the human population stayed the same. Prehistoric people lived by hunting and gathering until about 10,000 years ago.

Some Aboriginal people of Australia still have the knowledge to survive by hunting and gathering, just as their ancestors did thousands of years ago.

Hunters and gatherers, both in the past and today, know how to find food in the wild. Knowing how to control fire is also important so food can be cooked.

is ancient cave
inting shows a
nting scene.
ehistoric people
nted large
imals and
all prey.

Farmers

Why prehistoric people started to farm is not clear. Most scientists believe that the climate became warmer so animals migrated less. Some people started to settle in villages. They no longer had to travel great distances to find their next meal, so they had more time to experiment with farming. They gradually discovered that animals such as sheep and goats could be controlled. They learned that they could grow certain fruits and berries from seeds.

Stone Age Lifestyle

Skara Brae is a Neolithic village in the Orkney Islands, off northern Scotland. The well-preserved stone house shown at lower right contains stone furniture, such as beds and dressers. The inhabitants of Skara Brae farmed, fished, and hunted. Around 2500 B.C., the village was covered by sand, which preserved most of it until it was discovered after a storm in 1850.

People now had more time to care for larger families. They could build more permanent homes. If the growing season was a good one, they could trade their **surplus** crops with hunters and gatherers.

Modern recreation of a Stone Age village

17

Traders

With the shift to farming, people needed some different tools. Plows were invented, so larger areas of land could be cultivated. People still made simple tools and weapons from stone, however, as well as clay pots and various items from animal skins. They traded these goods with close neighbors. Through travelers, there was also some trade with people who lived far away. Trading centers developed. There, people not only traded their goods but met others from different tribes.

The development of trading allowed people to exchange information and gain new farming and **handicraft** skills. Some people even discovered that they could trade materials for labor.

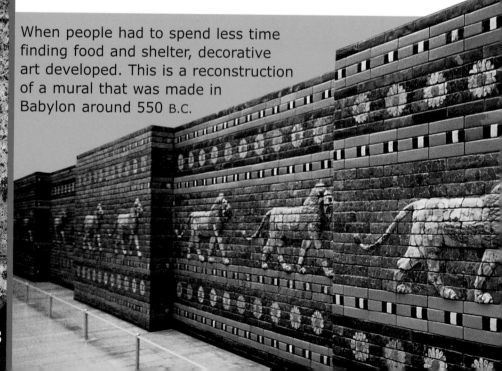

When people had to spend less time finding food and shelter, decorative art developed. This is a reconstruction of a mural that was made in Babylon around 550 B.C.

It is most likely that writing first developed so that people could keep business records! Records of property ownership, marriages, and wills were kept on clay tablets. Money did not yet exist so people paid for goods or services in grain, wool, or handicrafts.

Someone shaped this stone into a human figure about 5,000 years ago.

19

A Place in Time

Ten thousand years ago, people lived by hunting, fishing, and gathering food. They traveled from place to place, following the best food sources.

Four thousand years ago, many people settled in villages. They grew crops and kept animals. They had skills such as pottery-making, weaving, and metalworking.

Two and a half thousand years ago, technology had improved. People made tools and weapons of iron. They traded goods with other towns and villages.

The Rise of City-States

Coming Together

Farming and trade were two of the elements needed to create the first cities. The third element was location. Farming was a difficult way of life and required plenty of water and good soil. Traveling long distances to trade was difficult for farmers, so it made sense to live, farm, and trade in the same area.

By about 3500 B.C., many people had gathered together to live in permanent settlements in a number of river valleys. These small towns gradually became larger and more complex until they had grown into **city-states**. Each city-state had its own king and laws and was like a separate country. City-states often fought over land and access to water. Science and arts such as architecture, music, and literature developed in these **civilizations**.

Games were as popular in the ancient world as they are today. Archaeologists have found dice and board games at many ancient sites.

Scientists use a process called **carbon** dating. This process measures the amount of carbon in an object. Using this information in a special formula, scientists can calculate how old an object is. The object must be less than 50,000 years old, however, as carbon disappears over time, and an object older than this would have no carbon in it at all.

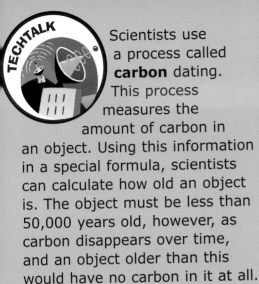

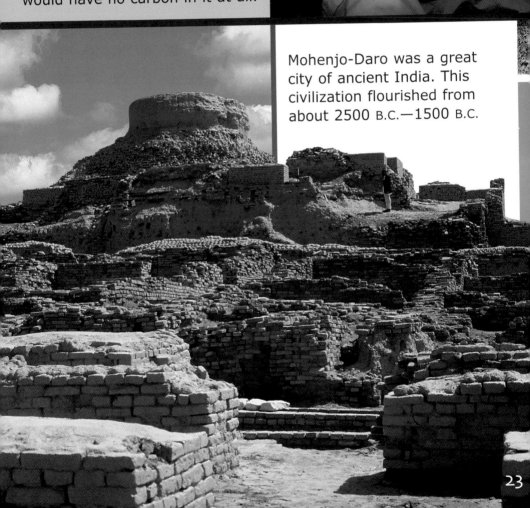

Mohenjo-Daro was a great city of ancient India. This civilization flourished from about 2500 B.C.—1500 B.C.

The Fertile Crescent

Most **historians** agree that the first cities grew up about 5,000 years ago in Egypt and in an area between Egypt and the Persian Gulf known as the Fertile Crescent. Early civilizations developed along major rivers because rivers provided water for farmland and a simple way of transporting people and materials to trade.

One of these civilizations started in Mesopotamia (now Iraq) between the Euphrates and Tigris rivers. The people who lived there were called the Sumerians. The Sumerians built many city-states, some with populations of up to 50,000 people. The Sumerian civilization was later conquered by the Akkadians, who were in turn conquered by the Babylonians. By 600 B.C., Babylon was the most important city in Mesopotamia.

WORD BUILDER

The name *Mesopotamia* means "between the rivers" in ancient Greek.

Two Assyrian kings shake hands in this stone carving.

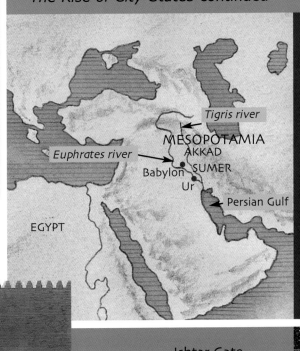

Tigris river

MESOPOTAMIA
AKKAD
Euphrates river
Babylon
SUMER
Ur
Persian Gulf

EGYPT

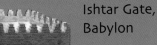

Ishtar Gate, Babylon

Daily Life in Mesopotamia

The Sumerians built great temples called **ziggurats**. Each city had one, and daily life was controlled by the high priests of these temples. Many people farmed lands owned by the temple and received food in payment for their work. If they were lucky, there would be some food left to trade.

Most children spent their days working in the fields. However, there were schools for boys, if their parents could afford to send them. Individuals who learned to read and write could become priests, writers, or merchants, but there was little opportunity for most people.

This ziggurat, in the Sumerian city of Ur, has been restored.

We can learn a lot about Sumerian society from this mosaic that was found in a royal tomb. The people in the top illustration are wealthy. They are enjoying themselves and listening to music.

The middle illustration shows people with **domestic** animals, fish, and other food.

The lowest illustration shows people transporting goods to the city.

27

Contributing to the Future

Imagine life without wheels! The Sumerians invented the wheel. In fact, we can thank the Sumerians for an amazing number of contributions to civilization. They invented the first twelve-month calendar, based on the cycle of the moon. This allowed people to calculate each growing season. The Sumerians developed mathematics to measure land area accurately. They had a counting system based on 60. Modern timekeeping developed partly from this—there are 60 seconds in a minute and 60 minutes in an hour.

However, the Sumerians are not the only early civilization to which we owe a debt. Other ancient civilizations also had ideas, made important discoveries, and invented tools and systems that we still use, in one form or another, today.

This model of a wagon was made about 2000 B.C. It was probably a child's toy.

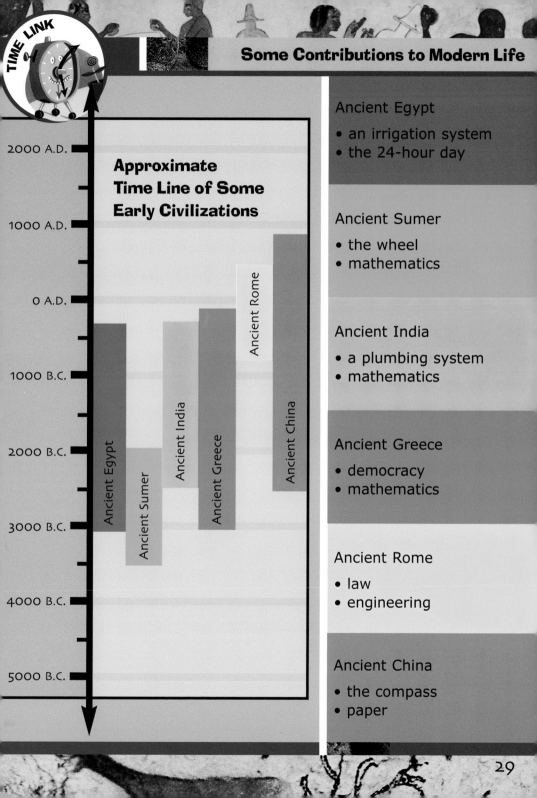

**Approximate
Time Line of Some
Early Civilizations**

2000 A.D.

1000 A.D.

0 A.D.

1000 B.C.

2000 B.C.

3000 B.C.

4000 B.C.

5000 B.C.

Ancient Egypt

Ancient Sumer

Ancient India

Ancient Greece

Ancient Rome

Ancient China

Ancient Egypt
- an irrigation system
- the 24-hour day

Ancient Sumer
- the wheel
- mathematics

Ancient India
- a plumbing system
- mathematics

Ancient Greece
- democracy
- mathematics

Ancient Rome
- law
- engineering

Ancient China
- the compass
- paper

Glossary

carbon – a chemical element that is found in coal and diamonds, and in all plants and animals

city-state – a city and its surrounding area that has its own laws and is independent

civilization – a highly organized society with government, culture, technology, and art

domestic – to do with the home. Domestic animals are tamed and are kept for food or as pets.

handicraft – an object made by hand

historian – a person who studies and writes about history

ice age – a time when the world's climate was much cooler than it is now and large sheets of ice covered many land areas, including North America. The last ice age is thought to have ended about 11,500 years ago.

prehistoric – the time before recorded history. Prehistoric people lived before the development of writing.

surplus – the amount left when what is needed has been used

ziggurat – a tall, rectangular tower with large steps, made of mud bricks. Ziggurats were used as temples by the Sumerians.

Index

Research Starters

1 Many cartoons show cave dwellers and dinosaurs together. Was this possible? Find out when dinosaurs lived and died.

2 For a long time, prehistoric people were hunters and gatherers. Then about 10,000 years ago, some of them began to farm. For what reasons might they have changed their way of life?

3 Mesopotamia has been called "the cradle of civilization" because Sumer, the first city-state, was established there. Find out about other ancient city-states in Mesopotamia.

4 Woolly mammoths and saber-toothed tigers are animals that lived in prehistoric times. Find out more about them. When did they become extinct, and why?